ESTHER,
GOD'S SPIRITUAL GANGSTER,

Antoinette Barnwell

WESTBOW
PRESS®
A DIVISION OF THOMAS NELSON
& ZONDERVAN

WestBow Press books may be ordered through booksellers or by contacting:

WestBow Press
A Division of Thomas Nelson & Zondervan
1663 Liberty Drive
Bloomington, IN 47403
www.westbowpress.com
844-714-3454

Because of the dynamic nature of the Internet, any web addresses or links contained in this book may have changed since publication and may no longer be valid. The views expressed in this work are solely those of the author and do not necessarily reflect the views of the publisher, and the publisher hereby disclaims any responsibility for them.

Any people depicted in stock imagery provided by Getty Images are models, and such images are being used for illustrative purposes only. Certain stock imagery © Getty Images.

Scripture taken from the King James Version of the Bible.

Scripture quotations taken from The Holy Bible, New International Version® NIV® Copyright © 1973 1978 1984 2011 by Biblica, Inc. TM. Used by permission. All rights reserved worldwide.

ISBN: 978-1-6642-7087-9 (sc)
ISBN: 978-1-6642-7088-6 (e)

Print information available on the last page.

WestBow Press rev. date: 07/29/2022

CONTENTS

INTRODUCTION

Our current world is filled with chaos.

Violence, racism, immorality, and selfishness, are operating at their highest level.

Causing many people, including Christians, to feel immense uncertainty and hopelessness.

Our spiritual enemy, Satan, also known as the devil, knows that his time on the earth is short, and the return of Jesus Christ to rapture his church is close.

He's camouflaging himself through demonic spirits of addiction, depression, and suicide, to decieve and destroy God's people.

Through spirits of pornography and lust, he's destroying Godly marriages.

He's stealing the God given dreams and visions that you and I have for our families, through spirits of greed, and discontentment.

Causing parents to work multiple jobs, to earn extra money.

In the process, families are being neglected, and Satan is gaining direct access into their lives.

At the end of the day, we're left feeling physically burned out, emotionally bankrupt, unsatisfied, and unfulfilled.

Satan's main agenda is to try to stop us from fulfilling our God given destiny and purpose, and to hinder the Kingdom of God from progressing forward through us.

God tells us in his word, that Christians don't have to accept the devil's mess, or conform to the negative standards of this world.

The current condition of our world, should cause a holy indignation to rise up on the inside of Christians.

Provoking a fervent and passionate zeal, that brings change, and serves Satan notice, that he can't have our families, our marriages, and our God given dreams.

John 10:10, (KJV),

States,

The thief cometh not but for to steal, and to kill, and to destroy: I come that they might have life, and that they might have it more abundantly.

Jesus Christ didn't die for us to live our lives filled with fear, defeat, and despair.

In addition, he gave Christians; blood washed believers in Christ, spiritual authority over Satan.

When Christians walk in their spiritual authority, using their spiritual weapons of prayer, fasting, praise, and intercession to combat him, his kingdom will be destroyed.

It's time for Christians to put up or shut up, because the spiritual warfare we're fighting against, will no longer allow us to sit on the sidelines being passive, and politically correct.

Agreeing with the twisted morals, values, and negative mindsets of our society, that's being proclaimed by the world as truth.

Every immoral view, and negative mindset, that's contrary to the word of God, came directly from Satan; the father of lies.

(Matthew 11:12), (KJV),

States,

And from the days of John the Baptist until now, the kingdom of heaven suffereth violence, and the violent take it by force.

Christians must become "Spiritual Gangsters" in the sense of pledging an allegiance and commitment to the covenant and personal relationship they have with God, through his son, Jesus Christ.

Our minds must be renewed daily with the truth of God's word, and consistently applied to our lives.

We must claim our family members and loved ones as territory, the devil can't have.

By vigilantly keeping watch over them, encouraging them and making them feel loved, whenever they're feeling discouraged from life's disappointments.

Reassuring them that the same God who loved us, extended his grace and mercy towards us, gave us his free gift of salvation, with total restoration, wants to, and will do the same thing for them.

Spiritual boldness and courage comes from knowing who we are in Jesus Christ.

Jesus' finished work on the cross, gives us the power to overcome Satan. An enemy whom we cannot see with our physical eyes, only with our spiritual eyes.

When we accept Jesus Christ, as our personal Lord and Savior, his Holy spirit comes to live on the inside of our heart.

Jesus, through the Holy Spirit, will govern and direct our lives, if we allow him to.

Through Jesus, we're empowered to do all things.

In his presence, spirits of fear and timidity, have to flee.

This is the story about Queen Esther, God's servant. A beautiful Jewish girl. Sent on an assignment from God, to appear before an earthly king and to request that he stop an evil plot, planned by one of his men, to destroy the Israelites. God's chosen people, and the lineage that would produce God's Son, Jesus Christ.

Queen Esther accepted and passionately pursued the call of God for her life. She held onto it like a piece of steak between the teeth of a bull dog's mouth, because she was determined to fulfill it.

She didn't let go of the purpose of God for her life, or give in to the temptation to quit, when things got hard.

With the fear of death staring her in the face, she boldly said to the devil and to all of hell, bring it!

Bring all you've got, because I'm going to do what God called me to do.

If I perish, I perish. (Esther 4:16), (KJV)

Her conscious decision saved her life, the destruction of her family and the extinction of the entire Jewish race.

There's no greater fight, than fighting for the betterment of our people and for the salvation of their eternal soul.

Queen Esther had "crazy" faith!

The kind of faith that prompted,fueled, and enabled her to be bold as a lion.

In the face of adversity and challenges, she answered God's call, and she did what was necessary to fulfill her purpose.

Jesus is praying, you and I do the same.

∞

CHAPTER 1

To See the Promises of God Fulfilled in our Lives, Will Require Christians to Have "Crazy Faith"

My definition of "crazy faith" is not having the kind of faith that's off the cuff, or reckless.

It's having the kind of faith that sounds crazy, and makes no sense to others, because it's not based on logic.

It's faith derived from having a track record with the true and living God.

Christians know him as abba father, or daddy.

I've experienced him, and know him to be a personal God.

He's my heavenly father.

The God who can reverse a negative doctor's report, put food on the table when your refrigerator is empty, make a way out of no way when your gas tank is empty, and the God who protects us in the midst of calamity.

He will comfort and hold you in his loving arms, when death comes and take our loved ones away.

He comforts us like no other can.

When the person closest to us, whom we thought would never leave, disappoint, and turn their backs on us, he will stick closer than a brother. (Proverbs: 18:24), (KJV)

Always fulfilling his promise, to never leave or forsake us. (Deuteronomy 31:8), (KJV)

Today, you may find yourself in a dire situation, resulting from a bad decision you made.

Maybe the prison that you're in, is an emotional or physical one, that's causing you to feel all alone and hopeless.

Whatever the circumstance or situation may be, I assure you that Jesus Christ is right there with you.

With him, there's always hope.

He can heal any hurt, and any pain you're experiencing.

He's waiting for you to invite him into your life, and into your heart.

Jesus loves you, and you're never too far gone for him to reach you, and to accept you as his child.

Don't believe the lies from Satan, or people, who may be trying to convince you otherwise.

The ingredients of "crazy faith" consists of, and comes through, experiencing the fiery trials of life.

I'm talking about the kind of trouble that knocks you to your knees, makes you pray, and call on the name of Jesus.

Jesus Christ, the Savior, and the only one who has the power to rescue and bring you out of whatever it is, you're going through.

Jesus Christ is a mind regulator, miracle worker, and the prince of peace.

He specializes in mending broken hearts, and broken lives.

I'm talking to you, mighty man of valor, and to you, powerful woman of God.

Pull yourself together, and rise up on the inside! From that low place that you're currently in.

You may not feel like doing it, but you can't quit now.

Your current situation is not how your story ends.

It's not over, until God says it's over!

Not when the "fat" lady sings.

God created you with purpose and destiny, and his plans for your life are good.

Not plans of destruction.

You must believe what God's word says about you.

His word says that you're more than a conqueror, and greater is he that is in you, than he that is in the world. (Romans 8:37), (KJV),(John 4:4), (KJV)

After you've experienced the good, the bad and the ugly in your life, and it seems you've been on a trip to hell and back, you'll reach a defining moment.

A place in your life where you're finally convinced, that you know, that you know, that you know, that you know, can't "NOBODY" do you like Jesus!

The depth of every trial and difficulty you experienced, makes your faith in Jesus Christ tangible and real, because your faith is ingrained and stamped on the inside of you, and it's now a part of who you've become.

This kind of faith will manifest itself on the outside of you, because it can't be contained.

It will be displayed through the faith filled words you speak, because they're no longer idle words, but words that are a part of your personal testimony.

They're words that's full of conviction and hope.

Not words of defeat, hopelessness, and despair.

When the trials of life came to test you, make you quit, and give up on your faith, you didn't quit or throw in the towel.

Maybe your faith was the size of a mustard seed, but it made you hold on to the promises of God.

Despite the opposition, you persevered, released your faith and you kept on fighting in the game of life.

You kept believing, until the thing you believed God for, came to pass.

"Crazy faith" brought you through your rough times and because you have faith that's built on a strong foundation, no one or nothing can ever take it away.

"Crazy faith" is acquired by knowing, believing, and trusting in Jesus Christ.

Faith in Jesus, makes us dream, and do the impossible. Even when the negative circumstances presented before us say, there's no way the thing that we're believing God for, will ever come to pass.

Joshua and Caleb, were two people in the bible whom God used mightily.

They both displayed the "crazy" faith that I'm talking about.

In the book of (Numbers, 13:1), (KJV),

God told Moses, their leader, to send twelve men, representing the twelve tribes of Israel, to go and spy out the land of Canaan, which God was giving to the Isrealites.

The spies mission was to report to Moses about the inhabitants of the land. (Numbers 13:17), (KJV)

Moses wanted to know, were the inhabitants many or few. (Numbers 13:18), (KJV)

What was the strength of the people occupying the land, and was the soil of the land fertile to grow crops? (Numbers 13:19), (KJV)

In addition, Moses instructed the spies to bring back fruit from the land. (Numbers 13:20), (KJV)

The twelve spies Moses sent, went and explored the land. (Numbers 13:21), (KJV)

After forty days, they came back and told Moses what they saw. (Numbers 13:25-26), (KJV)

They told Moses that the land they saw was very rich and fertile, and they brought back a cluster of grapes with them, which required two people to carry.

This was the promised land that God promised to give to his people, the Israelites.

The bible calls it, the land that flows with milk and honey, because it was full of God's favor and abundance. (Numbers 13:27), (KJV)

Ten of the spies said the people occupying the land are powerful and are descendants of Anak. (Numbers 13:28), (KJV)

Meaning they were giants, and very strong in stature.

Fear provoked ten of the spies to say to Moses, "we can't attack those people who are stronger than we are". "We seemed like grasshoppers in our own eyes, and we looked the same to them. " (Numbers 13:33), (KJV)

Then Caleb silenced the people and said, "we should go up and take possession of the land, we can certainly do it". (Numbers:13:30), (KJV)

This is a prime example of how a person's perception is everything.

Twelve spies saw the same thing, but only two of the spies, Joshua and Caleb, came to the positive and hopeful conclusion that, it didn't matter the size of the giants possessing the land, because the God whom they served was greater, and with God on their side, nothing, including this task, would be impossible for them to achieve.

Anytime God tells us to step out by faith, and do something that's a part of our God given destiny, Satan will always send the spirit of fear to try to stop us.

His lies may come in the form of a whisper in your ear, telling you that you're weak, you're not good enough, not smart enough and you'll never have the money, the resources, or know the right people to make your God given dreams a reality.

Life lessons have taught me that when God gives you a dream, his main requirement is that we believe him and don't doubt that he is faithful to equip us for the dream.

God will always prove to us that he's more than able, to provide everything that you and I need, to help us fulfill our purpose. Including the necessary resources, and the appropriate people we need.

Another person in the bible that exemplified "crazy faith", is the Apostle Paul, (a.k.a.), also known as, Saul.

The Apostle, Paul, was the epitome of a true gangster, in the negative sense.

Before Saul's personal encounter with the Lord, Jesus Christ, he arrested, jailed and murdered Christians, because he despised their message about Christianity. While traveling to Damascus, a blinding light consumed and blinded Saul, knocking him to the ground. (Acts 9:3-4), KJV

Suddenly, a blinding light consumed and blinded Saul, knocking him to the ground. (Acts 9:3-4), (KJV))

Jesus spoke to him saying, Saul, why are you persecuting me? Saul asked the Lord, why are you speaking to me? (Acts 9:5), (KJV)

The voice identified himself as Jesus. Jesus told him to get up and go to Damascus.

Once he got there, Jesus would further instruct him.

(Acts 9:8-9), (KJV)

For three days, Saul could not see.

The men traveling with Saul, led him into Damascus.

Saul later met a man in the city named Ananias.

Ananias laid his hands on Saul, and prayed for him. Restoring his sight. (Acts 9:17), KJV

While there, Saul was baptized, and he accepted Jesus Christ as his personal Lord and Savior.

After his conversion, God changed Saul's name to Paul.

For the sake of the Gospel of Jesus Christ, the Apostle Paul, suffered great persecution.

He was beaten, stoned, was shipwrecked, bitten by a snake, hungry, and put in jail. (2 Corinthians 11:25), (KJV), (Acts 28:3), KJV

He endured it all, and he never let go of his faith in Jesus Christ.

God used him to write a large portion of the bible's New Testament.

The Apostle, Paul, is responsible for winning countless souls for the kingdom of God.

If God could convert and use a previous murderer to do great and mighty things for his Kingdom, why can't he use you and I?

Some people would say because of Paul's past, he couldn't and shouldn't be used by God. How untrue, because God thought otherwise.

After Paul's conversion, he made a conscious decision to forget about his past mistakes, and he focused on God's purpose and calling for his life.

Phillippians 3:13, 14, (KJV)

States,

Brethren, I do not count myself to have apprehended: but this one thing I do, forgetting those things which are behind, and reaching forth unto those things which are before,

I press toward the goal for the prize of the upward call of God in Christ Jesus.

The same dogmatic zeal and tenacity that Paul used in the negative, to persecute Jesus Christ and his church, after his encounter with Jesus, he redirected and refocused his will to serve Jesus, in a righteous and positive way.

He became sold out to Jesus, and he devoted his life to furthering the gospel of Jesus Christ.

After we accept and receive Jesus Christ into our heart, we must do the same, because in Christ, we become new creations, and the old is passed away.

Don't ever feel or think that God can't use you or the bad things about your past life that you wished never happened, and that nothing good can happen because of them.

I'm a witness that God can, and he will use our former mistakes to set the captive free, because people can relate to someone who has experienced the same issues they've experienced, and to those who have been delivered and set free from their bondage, because of Jesus Christ.

After we receive God's forgiveness for our sins, we're supposed to tell others about what Jesus Christ did for us.

We must tell them how he loved us, and how he set us free from the bondage of sin and death.

People around us are yearning to hear the good news of hope, and restoration.

The gospel of Jesus Christ.

If you were a pimp back in the day, in your former life, before you had an encounter with Jesus Christ, now it's time to flip that around and be a pimp for Jesus. Go back to the "hood" and solicit your homeboys and homegirls. Tell them about the goodness of God in your life. How he turned your life around and that he will do the same for them.

Because on the corner in every neighborhood, or "the hood", there's a Pookie, Willie, and Shemeka, who doesn't know that Jesus loves them.

So much that he died for them.

If you were a former drug dealer before Jesus Christ saved you, and removed your desire to use and sell drugs, now it's time for you to work those business and management skills, to help promote the kingdom of God.

Go back and tell those people who were a part of your circle, that there's no high, like a "Holy Ghost" high!

Hallelujah!

Start serving in a bible based church, that's teaching God's word, and about the saving grace of Jesus Christ.

I assure you that every fragment of our lives, God will use, and he will waste nothing.

∞

CHAPTER 2

A Queen In The Making

In the third year of King Xerxes, who ruled over 127 provinces from India to Cush, King Xerses gave a banquet for his officials. (Esther 1:1), (KJV)

For numerous days, he displayed the great wealth of his kingdom and he held a banquet lasting a week. (Esther 1:4), (KJV)

The banquet was held in the garden of his palace, for all of the people in the Citadel of Susa. (Esther 1:5), (KJV)

The garden was decorated with beautiful colors of white and blue linen, purple material, and silver rings on marble pillars.

Some of the furniture inside of the garden was constructed of gold and silver, marble, mother of pearl and other expensive stones. (Esther 1:6), (KJV)

Wine was plentiful and served in gold goblets. (Esther 1;7), (KJV)

The king commanded each guest to drink as much as he wished.

Queen Vashti also gave a banquet for the women in the royal palace of King Xerxes. (Esther 1:9), (KJV)

On the seventh day, when King Xerxes was highly intoxicated, or in modern day vernacular, after he got turned up; (which means; to get loose and wild), from drinking his wine, he commanded the seven eunuchs who served him, to bring before him Queen Vashti, wearing her royal crown, to display her beauty to the people and nobles, because she was beautiful to look at.

(Esther 1:10-11), (KJV)

When the attendants delivered the king's request to Queen Vashti, she refused to appear before the king. (Esther 1:12), KJV

The King became very upset and angry with her. (Esther 1:13), (KJV)

He consulted his officials regarding Queen Vashti's behavior.

After their meeting, the King decided Queen Vashti's conduct would become known to all women, causing them to be disrespectful to their husbands. (Esther 1:18), (KJV)

The King issued a royal decree that Queen Vashti was never again to enter his presence. (Esther 1:19), (KJV)

He decided that Queen Vashti didn't deserve to be Queen, and he decided to give her position to someone else.

The King proclaimed that all women will respect their husbands, and that every man should be in charge of his own household. (Esther 1:23), (KJV)

Commissioners were appointed to choose beautiful young virgin girls throughout the province, to bring into the harem, at the citadel of Susa for the King. (Esther 2:2), (KJV)

Many girls, including Esther, were brought to the harem and assigned under the care of Hegai. (Esther: 2:8), (KJV)

Esther being included among the girls, and taken to the harem, was not by chance or accident.

God divinely and strategically chose her, and he allowed her to be in this specific place, at this time.

(Proverbs 20:24), (NIV),

States,

A person's steps are directed by the Lord. How can anyone understand his own way?

You and I make plans for our life, but God will order our steps.

(Matthew 22:14), (KJV)),

States,

For many are called, but few are chosen.

Those chosen by God are the people whom God knew by his infinite wisdom, would come to the realization and acknowledgement that they need a Savior, to save them from their sins. Because of the sin nature mankind inherited from Adam and Eve, when they disobeyed God, by eating the forbidden fruit in the garden of Eden.

The Holy Spirit, living through us, enables us to make a conscious decision to live a life that's Holy, righteous, and according to God's standard, the bible.

God's gift of salvation is a free gift and is available to everyone who will receive it.

Because God gave us the ability to choose, he will not force anyone to receive this free gift.

Queen Esther's humility, obedience, and willingness to serve God and people, allowed her to be used by God.

It's just like God, to take a young orphaned girl, with no notoriety and no experience, to complete a mighty task.

Because Esther's heart was pure, and she was an available vessel, God placed her in a position of great power and influence, and he chose to use her at a very crucial and pivotal time in history.

You may feel God prompting you to submit to his will for your life, but because you're not ready to submit to him, you keep running away, trying to avoid doing what you know he's called you to do.

It's time to stop running, and to completely surrender to God's will.

Surrendering to God's will, will allow you to experience a life that's filled with an abundance of joy, favor, and peace.

Despite the challenges you and I will face, on this Christian journey.

$$\text{\small ✶}$$

CHAPTER 3

Preparing to Meet the King

Before a girl could go into the presence of King Xerxes, intricate preparations were made.

(Esther 2:12), KJV,

The preparation consisted of twelve months of beauty treatments; six months with oil of myrrh, and six months with perfumes and cosmetics.

Anything she wanted was given to her, and she could take with her to the king's palace.

Hegai, the man placed in charge of the harem by the King, was pleased with Esther. (Esther 2:13), (KJV)

(Esther 2:9), (KJV)

He immediately began giving her beauty treatments, special food to eat, and he assigned her seven maids from the King's palace. He moved Esther and her maids into the best place in the harem.

If preparing to meet an earthly king was important by man's standards, how much more important is it that we prepare to stand before the righteous King of Kings, and the Lord of Lords, Jesus Christ?

Jesus Christ, the final judge, and the one who will judge unrepented sin.

(Genesis 2:7), (KJV)

States,

God formed our physical bodies from the dust.

He breathed life into us, and we became living beings.

Because we came from God, we will never die.

Immediately upon death, our physical bodies will return back to the dust from which it came, and the spirit that's on the inside of us, will leave our body.

God's angels, will immediately usher Christians; born again believers in Jesus Christ, into the presence of God.

Those who rejected God, and who choose not accept Jesus Christ as their personal Lord and Savior, before they died, will be escorted by God's angels, into the fires of hell, along with Satan and his fallen angels.

We must be prepared to stand in the presence of a righteous and Holy God.

We must be born again.

To be born again, requires that we repent by asking God to forgive us of our sins, and stop living our lives contrary to God's word.

We must also believe that Jesus Christ is the son of God, and his dying on the cross, on our behalf, paid the sin debt we owed to God in full, and that he rose from the grave on the third day.

It's as simple as that.

The trick of the devil is to make you and I wait, to try to fix our life, before we receive Jesus Christ as our Lord and savior, but we can't.

Today is the day of salvation. (2 Corinthians 6:2), (KJV)

Don't put it off. Tomorrow you may not have the chance.

❦

CHAPTER 4

God knows how to, and when to Expose our Enemies

The king was attracted to Esther more than the other women in the concubine.

He made Esther queen, instead of Vashti. (Esther 2:17), (KJV)

The king gave Esther a banquet and proclaimed it a holiday to celebrate her. (Esther 2:18), (KJV)

Esther had kept her nationality and family background a secret, at her cousin Mordecai's request. (Esther 2:20), (KJV)

Mordecai was afraid the king would not choose Esther as his wife, if he knew she was of Jewish descent. This truth was later revealed, after she became Queen.

One day when Mordecai was sitting at the king's gate, he heard two of the king's officers who gaurded the doorway, angrily conspiring a plot to murder the king, and he told Queen Esther about it. (Esther 2:21), (KJV)

Queen Esther told the king about the plot, he investigated it, and found it to be true. (Esther 2:22), (KJV)

The King had the two officials hanged on a gallows. (Esther 2:23), (KJV)

After this happened, King Xerxes, honored Haman, son of Hammadatha, the Agagite, giving him a position higher than all the other nobles. (Esther 3:1), (KJV)

All of the royal officials knelt and showed honor to Haman, but Mordecai refused to kneel down to show him honor. (Esther 3:2), (KJV)

The royal officials questioned Mordecai, wanting to know why he refused to bow down and to show Haman respect,and Mordecai never gave them a reason why. (Esther 3:3), (KJV)

The royal officials told Haman about Mordecai not bowing down to him, and they revealed to him the fact that Mordecai was a Jew. (Esther 3:4), (KJV)

(Esther 3:8-9), (KJV)

Haman became enraged and discussed the issue with the king.

He asked the King to make a decree to destroy Mordecai and all of the Jews. The old, the young, the men, women, and children, because of Mordecai's actions. (Esther 3:13), (KJV)

Haman also offered to pay the king money to put into the royal treasury, which the king declined.

The king honored Haman's request, and a law was issued by the king, to destroy the Jews. Every nationality was notified to prepare them for that day. (Esther 3:14), (KJV)

There's a saying in South Carolina where I'm from, that states: I would have loved to have been a "fly" on the wall, to hear the conversations of my enemies.

Just like God allowed Mordecai to be sitting at the palace gate, to hear the king's officials plotting to murder King, Xerxes, our heavenly father is omnipresent; meaning he's everywhere, at the same time, and he hears the conversations of his children's enemies.

God is that "fly on the wall.

He's more powerful than any source of intel that's manufactured in our world.

Scripture assures us that, God hears the plots, and the negative conversations of our enemies:

(2 Kings 6: 8-), (KJV)

States,

Now the king of Aram was at war with Israel. After conferring with his officers, he said, "I will set up my camp in such a place."

The man of God sent word to the king of Israel: "Beware of passing that place because the Arameans are going down there." (2 Kings 6:9), (KJV)

So the king of Israel checked on the place indicated by the man of God. Time and again Elisha warned the king, so that he was on his guard in such places. (2 Kings 6:10), (KJV)

This enraged the king of Aram. He summoned his officers and demanded of them, "Will you not tell me which of us is on the side of the king of Israel?" (2 Kings 6:11), (KJV)

None of us, my lord the king," said one of his officers, "but Elisha, the prophet who is in Israel, tells the king of Israel the very words you speak in your bedroom." (2 Kings 6:12), (KJV)

Go, find out where he is. "the king ordered, "so I can send men and capture him. (2 Kings 6:13), (KJV)

Here we see God giving his prophet divine insight regarding the enemy's plans.

God through the Holy Spirit, will always lead, guide and direct his children, in the way they should go. Our spirit must be in the right place, to discern what he's saying to us.

God is a loving, caring and compassionate father, but if you want to see him imitate a real "gangster", mess with, or try to hurt his children and you'll have to deal with him.

In (Exodus 14: 5-28),

After Pharaoh agreed to let God's people, the Israelites go, and set them free from the bondage of slavery, as they were leaving, Pharoah realized what he had done, and he had a change of heart. (Exodus, 14:5), (KJV)

Pharoah prepared his chariot and took his army with him. He took six hundred of his best chariots, as well as all the other chariots in Egypt, placing an officer in each of them.

The Egyptians pursued the Israelites, who were boldly leaving Egypt., (Exodus 14: 6), (KJV)

Pharaoh's army caught up with them, as they were setting up their camp by the sea at Pihahiroth. (Exodus 14:2), (KJV)

As Pharaoh approached, the Israelites looked up and saw that the Egyptians were coming after them. Terrified, the Israelites cried out to the Lord. (Exodus 14:10), (KJV)

They said to Moses, look what you've done by bringing us out of Egypt. (Exodus 14:11), (KJV)

Moses answered the people, "Don't be afraid! Stand still and see what the Lord will do to save you today. You will never see these Egyptians again. (Exodus 14:13), (KJV)

The Lord is fighting for you! So be still.", (Exodus 14:14), (KJV)

God told Moses to raise his staff, and to stretch out his hand over the sea, and the water. Then the Israelites will go through the sea on dry ground. (Exodus 14:16), (KJV)

The water stood like a wall, on their right and their left. (Exodus 14:22), (KJV)

The water flowed back and covered Pharaoh's entire army, his chariots, and the men that followed the Israelites into the sea. None of them survived. (Exodus 14:28), (KJV)

Pharoah and his men became fish food.

God said in:

(Romans 12:19),

Beloved, do not avenge yourselves, but rather give place unto wrath: for it is written, vengeance is mine; I will repay saith the Lord.

❦

CHAPTER 5

Queen Esther and Mordecai, Honored and Favored by God

(Esther: 4:1), (NIV),

When Mordecai heard about the fate of the Jews, he wept loudly and bitterly, in the city

(Esther: 4:4), (NIV)

Through one of the king's eunuchs, Mordecai informed Queen Esther of Haman's plans.

(Esther 4:9), (NIV),

Esther was reluctant to go before the king because, if any woman or man approached the king in the inner court, without being summoned by the king, the law required, they be put to death.

(Esther 4:11), (NIV),

There was one exception to this law; the king could extend his gold scepter, allowing the person to access him, and spare their life.

It had been awhile since the king requested to see Queen Esther.

(Esther 4:14), (NIV),

Mordecai informed her that if she remained silent, and not go before the king, to try to stop the annihilation of the Jews, deliverance would happen elsewhere, but she and her father's people would lose their life.

Mordecai told Esther, who knows, maybe you came to your royal position, for such a time as this.

(Esther 4:15-16), (NIV),

Esther called a fast for three days and three nights. After the fast, Queen, Esther, areed to go to see the king, even though it was against the law.

She said, "if I perish, I perish."

(Esther 5:1-2,), (NIV),

One day, the king saw Queen Esther, standing in the inner court of the palace, and he held out his gold scepter in his hand, and Esther touched the tip of the Scepter.

(Esther 5:3), (NIV)

The king asked her what she wanted. He offered to give her half of the kingdom if she wanted it.

(Esther 5:4), (NIV)

Queen Esther requested that the king and Haman come to a banquet she prepared.

(Esther 5:5), (NIV)

The king and Haman attended Esther's banquet.

(Esther 5:6), (NIV)

The king asked Queen Esther again, what was her request. Once again, he offered her half of the kingdom.

(Esther 5:7), (NIV)

Queen Esther's request was to have the king and Haman come back the next day, to attend another banquet prepared by her.

(Esther 5:8), (NIV)

Haman left the meeting feeling happy, until he saw Mordecai sitting at the king's gate, still refusing to bow to him, and he became angry.

(Esther 5:10), (NIV)

He went home bragging to his friends and to wife, about his great wealth, his sons, how the king elevated him above the other nobles, and the invitation to the banquet, from Queen Esther.

(Esther 5:13), (NIV)

Haman also told them about Mordecai sitting at the gate, refusing to bow to him.

(Esther 5:14), (NIV)

His wife and cousins suggested that he have gallows built, and have Mordecai hanged on it.

Haman had gallows built.

(Esther: 6:1-2), (NIV)

That night the king couldn't sleep; he ordered the book of the chronicles, the record of his reign, be brought and read to him.

It was recorded that, Mordecai had previously exposed the two guards, that conspired to murder the king.

The king asked his attendants, how was Mordecai honored for doing this, and the men said that nothing was done for him.

(Esther 6:4), (NIV)

The king asked who was in the court, and it was Haman in the outer court of the palace, coming to tell the king about the gallows he had built to hang Mordecai on.

(Esther 6:5), (NIV)

The king told the attendants to bring Haman to him.

(Esther 6:6), (NIV)

When Haman entered, the king asked him what should be done for the man the king desired to honor?" Haman wondered who the king wanted to honor, other than himself.

(Esther 6:7-9), (NIV)

So Haman answered the king, and said the king should;

Have them bring a royal robe the king has worn, and a horse the king has ridden, with a royal crest placed it's head.

Let the robe and horse be given to the king's most noble princes, and have him parade the man the king wants to honor, through the streets. Proclaiming before him, "This is what is done for the man the king delights to honor!"

(Esther 6:10), (NIV)

The king commanded Haman to go quickly and get the robe, and the horse, and do just what he suggested be done for Mordecai the Jew, who sits at the king's gate. The king told Haman to make sure he did everything that he recommended be done.

(Esther 6:11), (NIV)

Haman got the robe and the horse, and put the robe on Mordecai. He led Mordecai on horseback through the streets, proclaiming before him, "This is what is done for the man the king delights to honor!"

(Esther 6:12-13), (NIV)

Afterward, Mordecai returned to the king's gate, and Haman rushed home, with his head covered in grief.

Haman told his wife and friends what happened. They said to him, "Since Mordecai, before whom your downfall has started, is of Jewish origin, you cannot stand against him, you will surely come to ruin!"

(Esther 6:14), (NIV)

While they were talking, the king's eunuchs arrived and hurried Haman away to the banquet Esther had prepared.

(Esther 7: 1), (NIV)

The king and Haman went to Esther's banquet.

(Esther 7:2), (NIV)

The king asked Queen Esther, what was her request? Once again, he offered her half of the kingdom.

(Esther 7:3), (NIV)

Queen Esther answered, if I have found favor with you, please grant my life, this is my request and spare my people. This is my request.

(Esther 7:4), (NIV)

I and my people have been sold for destruction. If we had been sold as slaves, I would have kept quite, because that wouldn't warrant disturbing the king."

(Esther 7:5), (NIV)

King Xerxes asked Queen Esther, "Who is he?" Where is he? Who is the man who has dared to do such a thing?"

(Esther 7:6), (NIV)

Queen Esther said, Haman is the man. Haman was terrified before the king and queen.

(Esther 7;7), (NIV)

The king got up in a rage and went out into the palace garden. Haman realized the king had already decided his fate, so he began to beg Queen Esther for his life.

(Esther 7:8), (NIV)

The king's attendants covered Haman's face.

(Esther 7:9), (NIV)

One of the eunuchs attending to the king said," A gallows was constructed by Hamans's house. He had it built for Mordecai, who spoke up to help the king." The king said, "Hang him on it!"

(Esther 7:10), (NIV)

They hanged Haman on the gallows he had prepared for Mordecai.

(Esther 8:1), (NIV)

That same day, King Xerxes gave Queen, Esther, the estate of Haman.

Mordecai told the king how he was related to Queen Esther.

(Esther 8:2), (NIV)

The king took off his signet ring, which he had given to Haman and he gave it to Mordecai. Esther appointed him over Haman's estate. (Esther 8:3), (NIV)

The king's edict granted the Jews in every city the right to protect themselves; to destroy, kill and annihilate any armed force of any nationality or province that might attack them and their women and children; and to plunder the property of their enemies. (Esther 8:11), (KJV)

Esther pleaded with the king regarding the law that was written to destroy the Jews. (Esther 8:15), (NIV)

Mordecai left the king's presence wearing royal garments of blue and white, a large crown of gold and a purple robe of fine linen, and the city of Susa held a joyous celebration.

(Esther 9:13), (NIV)

Later in the story, a law was issued stating that the evil plot that Haman devised against the Jews, should transfer to his ten sons, and his sons were hanged on gallows.

(Esther 10:3), (NIV),

Mordecai the Jew, was second in rank to King Xerxes, preeminent among the Jews, and held in high esteem by many fellow Jews, because he worked for the good of his people and spoke up for the welfare of all Jews.

CHAPTER 6

Pain Gives Us the Necessary Grit and Stamina to Look Adversity in the Face with Attitude and Resilience, to Run and Finish this Christian Race

(Psalm 37:25), (KJV)

States,

I have been young and now am old; yet have I not seen the righteous forsaken, nor his seed begging bread.

Queen Esther experienced extreme pain in her life, before answering God's call.

Her parents died when she was young, making her an orphan, and having to be adopted by her cousin, Mordecai.

Esther also had to accept the fact of losing her parents and making the decision to keep living her life with uncertainty.

Since the Covid-19 pandemic started in March of 2020, many people have experienced extreme pain in their life, and have had to make major life adjustments.

From having to wear surgical face masks, conforming to mandatory self quarantine laws; to access businesses, losing multiple loved ones who contracted the coronavirus, have lost jobs they held for years, we've experienced basic necessity and food shortages and we couldn't attend worship services, due to the church doors being closed.

Pain connected to loss, can cause a person to experience emotional moments of anger, rage, blame, bitterness and asking God why.

God, why did I have to experience hardship, disappointment, and pain in my life?

This is a question we've all asked God, and we've had to accept the fact that we may never know why.

As long as we live, challenges, adversity and pain, will always come to test our faith, tempt us to quit and make us doubt God's love for us.

God reminds us in:

Psalms 34:19, (KJV),

States,

Many are the afflictions of the righteous; but the Lord delivereth him out of them all."

If you've ever worked out at the gym and lifted weights, you always start your weight training program with low weights, maybe three or five pounds, with repeated reps, of ten to twelve.

If your goal is to lift forty-five pounds to gain extra muscle, each time you go to the gym, you must increase the amount of weight that you're lifting.

As you increase the amount of weight that you're lifting, the resistance to lift the weight will seem like it's too much for you to handle, and you'll feel like you're going to die.

If you continue to be consistent, gradually, you'll reach your fitness goal and you'll become stronger.

This concept works the same way for us spiritually.

The trials, hardships, and difficulties we face, help to strengthen our spiritual muscles, and help build our faith.

No matter the doom and gloom we're hearing daily, that's coming from the news, and other media platforms, that's causing people to believe we're hopeless. I know without a doubt that God has not forsaken us, and he will always provide for his children.

It's time to turn off the negative noise, and to start meditating on the truth of God's word.

Instead of scrolling on social media platforms throughout the day, start scrolling on a bible app, to feed your spirit and help increase your faith.

(Romans 8:35), (NIV),

States,

Who shall separate us from the love of Christ?

Shall trouble or hardship or persecution or famine or nakedness or danger or sword?

(Romans 8:36), (NIV):

As it is written:

"For your sake we face death all day long;

we are considered as sheep to be slaughtered."

(Romans 8:37), (NIV):

No, in all these things we are more than conquerors through him who loved us.

(Romans 8:38- 39), (NIV):

For I am convinced that neither death nor life, neither angels nor demons, neither the present nor the future, nor any powers, neither height nor depth, nor anything else in all creation, will be able to separate us from the love of God. That is in Christ Jesus our Lord.

Right now, take a deep breath, and begin to rest in the promises of God, because God's got us!

(Matthew 6:25), (NIV)

"Therefore I tell you, do not worry about life, what you will eat or drink; or about your body, what you will wear. Isn't life more important than food, and the body more important than clothes?

(Matthew 6:26), (NIV)

Look at the birds of the air; they do not sow or reap or store away in barns, and yet your heavenly father feeds them. Are you much more valuable than they?

(Matthew 6:27), (NIV)

Who of you by worrying can add a single hour to his life?

(Matthew 6:28), (NIV)

And why do you worry about clothes? See how the lilies of the field grow. They do not labor or spin.

(Matthew 6:29), (NIV)

Yet I tell you that not even Solomon in all his splendor was dressed like one of these.

(Matthew 6:30), (NIV)

If that is how God clothes the grass of the field, which is here today and tomorrow is thrown into the fire, will he not much more clothe you, O you of little faith?

(Matthew 6:31), (NIV)

So don't worry, saying, What shall we eat? or What shall we drink?

or What shall we wear?

(Matthew 6:32), (NIV)

For the pagans run after all these things, and your heavenly father knows that you need them.

(Matthew 6:33), (NIV)

But seek first his kingdom and his righteousness, and all these things will be given to you as well.

(Matthew 6:34), (NIV)

Therefore do not worry about tomorrow, for tomorrow will worry about itself. Each day has enough trouble of its own.

$\mathcal{S}$

CHAPTER 7

Blood Washed Believers in Christ, Can't Allow the Devil to "Roll Up" on Them", and Steal Away their God Given Promises

To "roll up" on someone is a statement or term that's used in the ghetto, or in the hood; (the neighborhood).

It means to appear before someone without permission, or to show up before them unannounced.

If the "po,po" or the police were going to "roll up" on a drug lord living in the hood, they would have a strategy plan.

Possibly consisting of months, and maybe years, of monitoring the drug Lord's daily activity, because they'd want to be prepared.

They wouldn't just show up unannounced to take the drug lord down, without knowing the details of what they could be facing.

They also wouldn't send a new rookie on the force, to take the drug lord out, but they'd send their most experienced men.

The SWAT Team; (men who have specialized training in sensitive situations), would be the ones showing up at the drug lord's door, using the most advanced weapons that money could buy, to take them out.

The devil has observed everything about you and I, since the day we were born. He knows our weaknesses, and the things to use to get us off course and off of God's plan for our life.

Ephesians 6:12, States,

For we wrestle not against flesh and blood, but against principalities, against powers, against the rulers of darkness of this world, against spiritual wickedness in high places."

The evil spirits that's apart of Satan's demonic forces, have order and rank, that's similar to our armed forces, the military.

In 2022, Satan is no longer commanding his demon emps; (his low ranking demon spirits), but he's commanding his prized generals; (his high ranking demons), to attack and destroy Christians.

Christians have nothing to fear, because Jesus lives on the inside of every born again believer.

Christians, walking in their spiritual authority, have power over satan, and over all demonic spiritual forces.

(1 John 4:4) (KJV),

States,

Greater is he that is in us, than he that is in the world.

Before Queen Esther "rolled up" on the king, she knew that she needed to strategize, and to seek God for his guidance, because of the great task she faced.

Her powerful strategy included; prayer and fasting.

Spiritual fasting means to: Give up food or something we enjoy doing, to direct our focus on God.

It could be not eating certain foods we love to eat, not watching tv or spending time on social media, for a certain amount of hours a day.

Most people, while fasting, will pray to God, and listen to praise and worship music.

Fasting helps to draw us closer to God and gives us the spiritual discernment and mental clarity we need, to hear what God is speaking to our spirit.

By denying our flesh, and not giving it what it wants, it keeps us humble before God.

Prayer is the way we communicate with God.

We pray to God because we can't live our lives successfully without him.

We pray to God because he literally owns everything, including the very breath we breathe and if he chose to take it, there would be nothing we could do.

Prayer consists of us asking God to provide our daily needs, to protect us, and to lead and guide us in the way he will have us to go.

We want to live our life according to God's perfect will for our life, not his permissive will.

God won't force his children to choose his will, but when we're disobedient and we choose to live our life our way, we will never experience his best for us.

The time Queen Esther spent seeking and praying to God, made her courageous, bold and fierce, and enabled her to approach the king with power and authority.

As she approached the king, I envisioned her speaking no words.

The confidence and boldness she exuded, gave notice to her spiritual and physical enemies, that she was on a personal mission for God.

In her heart, she knew that God almighty; the I am, that I am, was sending her to complete this task, and because God sent her, he would be with her.

I'm talking about the same God that told Moses to go to Pharaoh and to tell him to let his people, the Israelites go.

Moses initially gave God several reasons why he couldn't do what God told him to do, because he felt he wasn't equipped to handle the immense assignment.

When Moses asked God whom shall I say sent me, God said to him, tell Pharaoh, I am, that I am sent you.

Simply put, God was telling Moses that he would be everything that Moses needed him to be.

Today, God is saying the same thing to you and I, and to every born again, blood washed believer in Christ.

The devil can only defeat us, when we don't know our identity in Christ, and if we're not confidently walking in that identity.

If our spiritual lives are shaky and built on a weak foundation, because we don't know that the promises of God belong to us, the devil will always be successful at defeating us.

Satan knows if we really believe in the Jesus we're professing and if we truly believe or not, that the promises of God are ours to possess.

Just like the story of the seven sons of Sceva, the sons of a Jewish priest. In;

(Acts 19:11-20), KJV

The men tried to cast evil spirits out of a demon possessed man, declaring the name of the Lord Jesus, whom the Apostle, Paul preached.

The evil spirit inside of the man answered them saying, "Jesus I know and Paul I know, but who are you?"

The man who had the evil spirit jumped on the seven men and overpowered them. He beat them so badly, they ran out of the house naked and bleeding.

The devil is no fool, and he knows if we're pretending to be Christians on Sunday and not living the life of one, the rest of the week.

When we're walking in our spiritual authority, and the devil tries to "roll up"on us, to steal the promises of God away from us, we must let him know that our identity is in Jesus Christ, and his finished work on the cross.

We must use our spiritual authority to rebuke him, by speaking the truth of God's word.

He will try to intimidate us by using the spirit of fear against us.

FEAR:

When he "rolls up"on us using the spirit of fear, remind him of

(2 Timothy 1:7), (KJV))

That states,

For God has not given us a spirit of fear, but of power and of love and of a sound mind.

SICKNESS:

When the devil "rolls up" on us by sending sickness to rob us of our health, don't just sit there and entertain the negative thoughts spoken through a negative doctor's report, or spoken by your family members and friends.

Tell Satan and remind yourself, that healing is a part of a born again believer, a child of God, spiritual inheritance.

It doesn't matter what the physical symptoms say.

Believe and claim God's word, until you're walking in the full manifestation of his promise.

(Isaiah 53:5), (KJV)

States,

He was wounded for our transgression, he was bruised for our iniquities: the chastisement of our peace was upon him; and with his stripes, we are healed.

FINANCES:

Sooner or later, the devil will "roll up" on our bank account, and cause our money to look a little funny.

When we honor God with our finances, the following bible verse belongs to us.

(Malachi 3:10), (KJV)

States,

Bring ye all the tithes into the store house, that there may be meat in mine house, and prove me now here with, saith the Lord of hosts, If I will not open you the windows of heaven, and pour you out a blessing, that there shall not be room enough to receive it.

FAMILY:

If the devil can't cause us to stumble and live a life that's contrary to God's word, he will work overtime to keep our unsaved family members blinded from God's truth.

When he "rolls up on " our unsaved family members,

That's the time for those praying moms, dads, grandparents and disciples of God, to say, back off devil because you're messing with the wrong one.

That one belongs to God and you can't have them!

I don't care how our family members may be acting right now, and how far they seem to be from God's reach,we must never stop praying and interceding to God on their behalf, for their salvation.

God promised us in his word, that our entire household will be saved.

Pray until something happens, because God hears our prayers and he knows how to reach our lost family members.

In his time, our prodigal sons, daughters, and family members, will come home.

(Acts 16:31), (KJV)

States,

And they said, "Believe in the Lord Jesus Christ, and thou shall be saved, and thy house."

$$\propto$$

CHAPTER 8

Spiritual Gangsters for Christ, Must be Spiritually and Physically Fit to Fight the Good Fight of Faith

(3 John 2:5), (KJV)

States,

Beloved, I wish above all things that thou mayest prosper and be in health, even as thy soul prospereth.

When we receive Jesus Christ as our personal Lord and Savior, we inherit spiritual and physical blessings.

Our soul prospers when we read God's word daily.

In the physical, we can't prosper and be in good health, when we neglect and abuse our physical bodies, by not getting the proper amount of sleep, taking the proper vitamin supplements, eating healthy foods and exercising regularly.

When we abuse our bodies, they will eventually break down and become susceptible to disease, and they will not perform the way that God designed them to function.

This is a very sensitive subject for church folks.

Because we can praise God, shout, speak in tongues and do church, but please don't mess with our food.

Especially when most of us grew up in families, who didn't have much to give, or share with anyone.

When it came to preventing anyone from going hungry, our moms, grandmoms and aunties always found a way to share the little food they had.

Different cultures eat different foods for their Sunday dinner, but most families from the hood, can relate to the Sunday dinners my family and I ate in South Carolina that included; collard or mustard greens, cooked with pigtails and ham hocks, macaroni and cheese, white rice, fried chicken, cornbread or biscuits, loaded with lots of butter and syrup dripping from it, with a big glass of sweetened tea or kool-aid, and made with so much white processed sugar, it made your head hurt after you drinked it.

Not to mention, topping it off with our mom, grandma and our aunts' famous sweet potato pie or cake.

Because you could feel the love that was put into cooking the food, and how good the food tasted, it made you wiggle your toes after eating each bite, and it made you want to do a happy dance.

Shortly after, the only thing you felt like doing was, to go to sleep and take a nap.

What a time! What a time!

Food has always been a great tool to bring families close together, but when we abuse it by using it as comfort food, and as a form of gluttony, to mask and feed our emotional pain, the devil will use it as a way to access our lives to destroy us, and we won't experience the prosperous life in our health, that Jesus Christ died to give us.

If we're overweight and sick from overeating and from not eating healthy foods to properly nourish our bodies, and keep us physically strong and fit, God can't be glorified through our lives.

The world's definition of a prosperous life does not include God's definition, because it's centered around having money and things.

The rich and famous people in our world are quick to proclaim that they're selfmade.

Not wanting to associate God, or give him credit for any part of their success.

The world's definition of prosperity is all about obtaining as much stuff you can get, by stepping on whomever you need to step on to get it, no matter the cost, and spending a lifetime of anxiety and toil, without peace, to keep it.

If Christians are going to be "Spiritual gangsters" for Christ in every aspect of our lives, we must emulate God's definition of prosperity.

God desires for his children to be prosperous in every area of their life.

This includes; having prosperity in our bodies or our health, our emotions, our spirit, our relationships and our finances.

God owns everything, and we're only stewards of the things he allows us to have.

It is God who gives us the power to create wealth, to establish his covenant in the earth. (Deuteronomy 8:18), (KJV)

When our hearts are pure, with a will to live a righteous life before God, he will bless our lives to be a blessing to others, and we'll continually experience and walk in his definition of true prosperity.

No matter the state of our worlds' economy.

When Christians are walking in, and experiencing God's definition of a prosperous life, it will be evident to the world, because there will be a great distinction between the world, and the church, that can't be denied.

God wants and needs his people to be healthy and strong; spiritually, physically and mentally, to fulfill the assignment he's given us.

Until Jesus Christ returns, there will be kingdom work to do, inside and outside of the church walls.

Enough of the excuses because Christians are not only being defeated by the devil from a lack of feeding our spirit regularly, with the truth of God's word, but he's defeating us because of the bad choices we're making when it comes to taking care of our physical bodies; our temple, that house God's spirit.

We must learn to eat healthy. By not eating processed foods, foods made with preservatives, excessive sugar and excessive chemicals.

Before starting any exercise regimen, please consult your doctor, to ensure that you're healthy enough to.

If your doctor gives you the green light to start an exercise program, put those doughnuts and cookies down, get up off that chair and start moving that body, because our bodies weren't made for a sedentary lifestyle; to sit and do nothing all day. God created them to move.

If you can run, run. If you can't run, walk. If you like to dance, put on some zumba videos, or praise and worship music and start moving.

Make it fun, and include the entire family.

Try incorporating some resistance weight training in your workout program, because it will help you burn more fat calories.

You will begin to feel more energized, and more positive each day, and just like God said in;

(Psalm 103:5), (KJV)

Your youth will begin to be renewed like the eagle.

God's prosperity gives his children physical and spiritual renewal.

The total package, lacking nothing.

$$\infty$$

CHAPTER 9

God is Preparing a Place in Heaven for Blood Washed Believers in Christ; (A.k.a), The Spiritual Gangsters for Jesus Christ

Heaven is a prepared place for God's prepared people.

God's word assures us that heaven is a real place.

It doesn't matter if some people believe that it's just a figment of our imagination or not.

God said it in his word and that settles it.

The scripture in (John 14: 2-3), (KJV),

States,

In my Father's house are many mansions: if It were not so, I would have told you. I am going to prepare a place for you.

And if I go and prepare a place for you, I will come again, and receive you unto myself; that where I am, there you may be also.

If you and I live to be one hundred years old or more on this earth, it's nothing compared to eternity, because in eternity, time will never end.

The beauty of our current world is a copy of the beauty and splendor of what heaven will be like.

In this verse of scripture in, (Revelation 21:19-21), (NIV)

God allowed John the Baptist, to see a vision, to give us a glimpse of heaven and its beauty;

The foundations of the city walls were decorated with every kind of precious stone,

The first foundation was jasper, the second sapphire, the third agate, the fourth emerald, the fifth onyx, the sixth ruby, the seventh chrysolite, the eighth beryl, the ninth topaz, the tenth turquoise, the eleventh jacinth, and the twelfth amethyst.

The twelve gates were twelve pearls, each made of a single pearl.

The great street of the city was of gold, as pure as transparent glass.

You may have thought you've seen bling, bling, but only God knows how to make the real bling, bling!!

Our loved ones who died serving and believing in Jesus Christ, are in heaven, and are awaiting the day, when they will reunite with family members.

If you took your last breath on earth right now, and God called your name, do you know where you would spend eternity?

This is the most important question that you and I will ever answer.

They're only two destinations; Heaven or Hell.

There is no purgatory.

What place will be your destination?

If you're not making preparations to go to heaven, you won't make it there.

Don't get caught up and distracted by the things of this world,that will one day pass away, and have no spiritual meaning or importance.

The devil wants to use them, to keep you spiritually blinded, and enslaved by sin, and to keep your focus off of the things of God, and doing his will.

Today, start living your life with God's purpose, as priority in your life.

Never stop dreaming and living your life with expectation, hope, and believing in the goodness of God.

Who knows, you might be the one in your family, like Queen Esther, that God chooses to use, to ignite hope and bring change in their lives, and to our world.

Why not you?

(Nehemiah 8:10) (KJV)

Reminds us that the joy of the Lord is our strength, and his joy is not based on happy circumstances.

God's joy comes from knowing who we are in Jesus Christ, and the personal relationship that we have with him.

We should leave a legacy that gives hope, and inspiration to our families and to our world.

Our lives should be so pleasing to Jesus Christ, that it draws our family members, and those we encounter, into a personal relationship with him.

God is counting on us to leave a legacy that's powerful. So powerful, that it crushes the devil's kingdom, and wins countless souls for Jesus Christ.

God bless.

CHAPTER 10

Acknowledgements

My heavenly father, I thank you for being my father, I thank you for the gift of life, I thank you for loving and accepting me, and for sending your precious son, Jesus Christ to die for me.

To my husband, Victor L. Barnwell, thank you for loving me unconditionally and for always having my back. I love and I'm blessed to have you in my life.

Thank you to my children: Jerry (JC), and Blair, for loving me. I'm so grateful that God gave you to me, to love.

To my grandchildren: Jaylen, Kaylix and Malik, I love you all and you're very precious to me.

To my parents, Woodrow W. Cochran, and Helen L. Cochran, thank you for your many sacrifices and for the gift of life.

I love you and may the blessings of God overtake your life.

A special thank you to my in-laws, Joseph and Martha Barnwell.

I love you both and I'm grateful to God for you.

Thank you to my Spiritual Parents, Pastor, Rogerstine Gourdine, and Sister Nancy, for the spiritual seeds you sowed into my life.

The Applied Word Ministry will always be my home.

May God continue to bless your lives. I love you both.

Thank you to my sisters, Jeanette, Sandra and Shayla. I love and appreciate you all.

Thank you to my brother-in-law, aunts, uncles, nieces, nephews, cousins, extended family members, and friends, for your love and support.

Thank you to Alex, Dom, Mila, Maleah, Victoria, Chapa and Leya, for your love and encouragement. I love you all.

Thank you, thank you, thank you, to my New Covenant Christian Fellowship Church family.

It's such a joy serving with you all. May God continue to bless your lives.

The people that God used to encourage and impart wisdom into my life, (you know who you are). Thank you for being obedient to God, and for blessing my life with your unconditional love and presence.

I love you and God bless you.

Jason Abbott, thank you for your kindness, support and witty sense of humor. You're a joy to work with and I'm grateful and blessed to have a friend like you.

Lisa Bella Ramsey and your amazing assistant, Eliza, thank you for always providing exceptional customer service. No matter the occasion, you always work magic with those makeup brushes. I'm truly blessed to have you both in my life.

Printed in the United States
by Baker & Taylor Publisher Services